Paperback ISBN: 978-1-956870-05-3

READING GUIDE FOR THE HINDI AND ENGLISH IDIOMS

Every page has a Hindi and English idiom. Right below the Hindi idiom is the phonetic translation, followed by the literal translation of the words (color coded) to help kids recognize Hindi words. This is followed by the meaning of the idiom. The images and sentence showcase some Indian festivals and their respective traditions celebrated January through December. Relatable situations help provide context to the idioms as they could be used in daily conversation.

ज़मीन आसमान एक करना

Zameen aasmaan ek karnaa

Doing ground and sky one

Meaning - Doing hard work to achieve something

English Idiom : Leave no stone unturned

मकरसंक्रांति मनाने के लिए बच्चों ने पतंग बनाने में ज़मीन आसमान एक कर दिया।

Makarsankranti manaane ke liye bacchon ne patang banaane mein zameen aasmaan ek kar diya.

To celebrate Makarsankranti kids left no stone unturned when making the kites.

2 ✓

एक से भले दो

Ek se bhale doh
Two are better than one
Meaning - More minds can always help solve a problem
English Idiom : Two heads are better than one

पापा को लोहरी की आग जलाने में मुश्किल हो रही थी। रोहन और लकड़ी लेकर आया, मदद की और बोला, "एक से भले दो।

Papa ko Lohri ki aag jalaane mein mushkil ho rahi thi. Rohan aur lakdee lekar aaya, madad ki aur bola, "Ek se bhale do."

Father was having trouble lighting the Lohri fire. Rohan brought more wood, helped and said, "Two heads are better than one."

गई भैंस पानी में

Gayi Bhains Pani Mein

Buffalo went in water

Meaning - When someone works hard at something but with no results

English Idiom - All efforts have gone in vain

होली पर पापा बहुत देर से अपना सफ़ेद कुर्ता बचा रहे थे। जैसे ही घर के बाहर निकले तो बच्चों ने उनपर रंग डाल दिया। पापा बोले, "गयी भैंस पानी में।"

Holi par papa bahut der se apna safed kurtaa bachaa rahe the. Jaise hi ghar ke bahar nikale toh bachchon ne unpar rang daal diya. Papa bole, "Gayi Bhains Pani mein"

Father had been saving his white kurta for a long time on Holi. As soon as he came out, the children put color on him. Papa laughed, "All efforts went in vain."

चोर की दाढ़ी में तिनका

Chor ki daadhi mein tinka
Thief with straw in his beard
Meaning - Guilty person always reveals themselves
English Idiom - A guilty conscience needs no accuser

"मैंने ज़्यादा अंडे नहीं उठाये।" ओवेन ईस्टर मनाते हुए बोला। उसके चाचा हंसें, "चोर की दाढ़ी में तिनका। चलो, कुछ ईस्टर के अंडे वापस रखो। सबको बराबर मिलना चाहिए।"

"Maine zyada ande nahi uthaaye." Owen Easter manaate hue bola. Uske chacha hansein, "chor ki daadhi mein tinka. Chalo, kuch easter ke ande wapas rakho. Sabko barabar milne chahiye."

"I didn't take more eggs." Owen said while celebrating Easter. His uncle laughed, "Guilty conscience needs no accuser. Come, put some of the Easter eggs back. Everyone should get equal quantity."

पेट में चूहे कूदना

Pet mein chuhe **kudnaa**

Mice **jumping in** stomach

Meaning - Feeling very hungry

English Idiom : Stomach rumbling

मोहम्मद बोला, "रमदान में हर रोज़ इफ्तार के बिलकुल पहले ही क्यों पेट में चूहे कूदने लगते हैं?"

Mohammad bola, "Ramadaan mein har baar Iftaar ke bilkul pehle hi kyon pet mein chuhe kudne lagte hain?"

Mohammad said, "I don't know why during Ramadaan the stomach rumbles only right before Iftaar?"

मन में लड्डू फूटना

Mann mein laddoo futnaa
Ladoos bursting in the heart
Meaning - To be excited when thinking of something
English Idiom - Bubbling over with joy

ईद पर कितनी ईदी मिलेगी सोचकर बच्चों के मन में लड्डू फुट रहे थे।

Eid par kitnee Eidee milegi sochkar bacchon ke mann mein ladoo phut rahe the.

Kids were bubbling over with joy thinking about how much Eidee they would get on Eid.

Eid Mubarak

आँखों का तारा

Ankhon ka taara

Star of eyes

Someone beloved

English Idiom - Apple of one's eye

"कृष्ण कितनी भी बदमाशियां क्यों न करें, वो यशोदा की आँखों के तारे थे। हर माँ ऐसी ही होती है," नानी ने जन्माष्टमी पर कहा।

"Krishna kitne bhi badmaashi karein, woh Yashoda ki aankh ke taare the. Har maa aisi hi hoti hai," Nani ne Janmashatami par jhulaa jhulaate hue kahaa.

"No matter how much mischief Krishna did, he was the apple of Yashoda's eyes. Every mother is like this," Nani said on Janmashtami.

ऊंट के मुँह में जीरा

Oont ke **muh** mein **jeera**

Cumin in a camel's mouth

Meaning - A very small amount compared to the amount needed

English idiom - Drop in the ocean

जब माँ ने दर्शन के बाद बच्चों को एक-एक मोदक बांटा तो एक बच्चा बोला, "एक से मेरा क्या होगा? यह तो जैसे ऊंट के मुंह में जीरा।"

Jab ma ne darshan ke baad, bacchon ko ek modak baantaa toh, ek baccha bola, "Ek se mera kya hoga? Yeh toh jaise oont ke muh mein jeera."

When the mother distributed one modak each to the children after the darshan, one child said, "What will one do for me? This is like a drop in the ocean."

उतने ही पाँव पसारों, जितनी चादर
Utne paav pasaaron, jitni chaadar
Stretch your legs per your sheet
Meaning - Only spend according to your budget
English Idiom - Cut your coat according to your cloth

रक्षाबंधन पर जब दिवा ने और बड़ा उपहार माँगा तो माँ ने कहा, "भैया ने अपनी चादर के हिसाब से खर्चा किया है।थैंक यू बोलो। "

Rakshabandan par jab Diva ne aur bada uphaar manga Ma ne kahaa, "Bhaiyaa ne apni chaadar ke hisaab se kharacha kiya hai. Thank you bolo."

When Diva asked for a bigger present on Rakshabandhan mom said, "Your older brother has cut the coat per the cloth available. Just say thank you!"

एक हाथ से ताली नहीं बजती

Ek haath se taali nahin bajti

One hand cannot clap

Meaning - It takes two people to cause a quarrel

English Idiom - It takes two to quarrel

टीना ने राखी मनाने के बाद कहा, "भैया हमेशा लड़ाई करता है।" माँ ने कहा, "ताली एक हाथ से नहीं बजती। तूने क्या किया?"

Tina ne Rakhi manaane ke baad kahaa, "Bhaiyaa hamesha ladaayi kartaa hai." Ma ne kaha, "Taali ek haath se nahi bajti. Tune kya kiya?"

After celebrating Rakhi, Tina said, "Big brother always fights with me." Mom said, "It takes two to quarrel. What did you do?"

बूँद बूँद से सागर भरता है

Boond Boond se sagar bharta hai

Drop drop fills the ocean

Meaning - Small efforts can add up to big result

English Idiom - Little drops make the mighty ocean

"ओणम के लिए इतने पकवान कब बनाये?"दादी ने पूछा। माँ बोली, "बूँद-बूँद से सागर भरता है।"

"Onam ke liye itne pakwaan kab banaaye?" Daadi ne puchaa. Ma boli, "Boond boond se saagar bhartaa hai.

When did you cook all these delicacies for Onam?" Grandmother asked. Mom said, "Little drops make the mighty ocean."

नाच न आये आँगन टेढ़ा
Naach na aaye, Aangan tedha
Can't dance, the courtyard is tilted
Meaning - To not know how to do something so one makes excuses
English Idiom - Only a poor workman blames his tools

नवरात्रि पर गायत्री बोली, "ये डांडियां अच्छी नहीं हैं|" उसकी बेहेन बोली, "नाच न आये आँगन टेढ़ा। ऐसे करो."

Navraatri par Gaayatri boli, "Yeh Daandiyaan achchi nahi hai." Uski behen boli, "Naach na aaye aangan thedha. Aise karo."

On Navratri, Gayatri said, "These daandiya sticks are not good." Her sister said, "Only a poor workman blames his tools. Do like this."

बगल में छोरा, शहर में ढिंढोरा

Bagal mein chchora, shahar mein dhindora
Boy **standing close,** drums **far in** city
Meaning - Finding the thing or solution close by while we have been searching everywhere
English Idiom - Right under the nose

दशहरा मनाने के लिए पापा ने रावण का पुतला पुरे शहर में ढूंढा। माँ ने शाम को कागज़ की कठपुतली बनाकर कहा, "बगल में छोरा, शहर में ढिंढोरा।"

Dussehra manaane ke liye papa ne Raavan ka putlaa pure shahar mein dhoondha. Maa ne shaam ko kaagaz ki kathputlee banaa kar kahaa, "Bagal mein chchoraa, shahar mein dhindhora."

To celebrate Dussehra, Father looked all over the city for a Raavan effigy. In the evening, Mom made puppets with paper and said, "Right under our very nose."

घर सर पर उठा लेना

Ghar sar par utha lena

Lift the house on the head

Meaning - To throw a tantrum or make a lot of noise

English idiom - Blow a fuse

जब दिवाली की तैयारी समय पर शुरू नहीं हुई, माँ ने पूरा घर सर पर उठा लिया।

Jab Diwali ki taiyaari samay par shuru nahi hui, Ma ne pura ghar sar par utha liya.

When Diwali preparation didn't start on time, Mom blew a fuse.

आम के आम, गुठलियों के दाम

Aam ke aam, gutliyon **ke** daam

Mangos mangoes, **price** of mango seeds

Meaning - To get double benefit

English idiom - More bang for your buck

जब दिवाली पर घर साफ़ होता है तो बहुत सारी पुरानी चीज़ें मिल जाती हैं। इसे कहते हैं। आम के आम, गुठलियों के दाम।

Jab Diwali par ghar saaf hota hai toh bahut saari purani cheezein mil jaati hain. Isse kehte hain aam ke aam gutliyon ke daam.

During Diwali when house is getting cleaned, lots of old things are found. So much bang for your buck.

जैसा देश वैसा भेष

Jaisaa desh vaisaa bhesh

Like country, like clothes

Meaning - Dressing per the event or place

English Idiom - When in Rome, do as Romans do

रवि ने कहा उसको धनतेरस पर कुर्ता पैजामा नहीं पेहनना। माँ ने कहा, "पहन लो बेटा। जैसा देश, वैसा भेष।"

Ravi ne kaha usko Dhanteras par kurta pajama nahi pehenna. Ma ne kaha, "Pehen lo beta. Jaisa desh, vaisa bhesh."

Ravi said he doesn't want to wear kurta pajama for Dhanteras. Maa said, "Wear it darling. When in Rome, do as Romans do."

आँख दिखाना

Aankh dikhana

To show eyes

Meaning - To show your anger to someone

English Idiom - Give angry look

जब बच्चों ने मस्ती करते हुए रंगोली ख़राब कर दी।

Jab bacchon ne masti karte hue Rangoli kahrab kar di toh Ma ne aankh dikhaayi.

When the kids spoilt the Rangoli while running around, Mom gave them an angry look.

मुँह में पानी आना
Muh mein paani aana
Water in the mouth
Meaning - When something looks too delicious
English idiom - Mouth watering

दिवाली के पकवान देखकर, सेजल और तरन के मुँह में पानी आ गया।

Diwali ke pakwaan dekhkar, bacchon ke muh mein paani aa gaya.

Seeing Diwali treats, the kids' mouths started watering.

बाएं हाथ का खेल

Baayein hath ka khel
Left hand's game
Meaning - Easy job for someone
English Idiom - Child's play

निवेद ने गुजिया बनाने की कोशिश की तो उसने कहा, "कितना मुश्किल है यह। माँ के लिए तो यह बाएं हाथ का खेल है।"

Nived ne Gujiya banaane ki koshish ki toh usne kaha, "Kitna mushkil hai yeh. Ma ke liye toh yeh baayein hath ka khel hai."

When Nived tried making Gujiya, he said, "This is so difficult. For Mom this is child's play."

एक पंथ दो काज

Ek panth do kaaj
One stone two jobs
Meaning - To make the most of an opportunity
English Idiom - Killing two birds with one stone

पापा ने दिवाली की लाइट्स लगाई तो सेजल ताली बजाकर बोली, "ये लाइट्स तोह क्रिसमस तक चलेंगी। एक पंथ दो काज।

Papa ne Diwali ki lights lagaayi toh Sejal taali bajaakar boli, "Yeh lights toh Christmas tak chalegi. Ek panth do kaaj."

When dad put up the lights, Sejal clapped and said, "These lights can stay on till Christmas. That's killing two birds with one stone. "

सब्र का फल मीठा

Sabra **ka phal** **mithaa**

Patience **makes for** **fruit** **sweet**

Meaning - The wait makes for great rewards

English Idiom - Patience is a virtue

बच्चों ने जब पटाखे जलाने की ज़िद्द की तो पापा बोले, "सब्र का फल मीठा."

Bacchon ne jab pataakhe jalaane ki zidd ki toh Papa bole, "Sabra ka phal mitha."

When kids insisted to light the fireworks, Papa said, "Patience is a virtue."

चोर चोर मौसेरे भाई

Chor chor mausere bhai
Thief thief always cousins
Meaning - People with the same tastes and interests will be found together.
English Idiom - Birds of a feather, flock together

बच्चों ने दिवाली का त्यौहार मनाते हुए कहा, "काश कल छुट्टी होती है। क्या हम कल स्कूल नहीं जाएँ ? " मम्मी पापा हसें और बोले, "चोर चोर मौसेरे भाई।"

Bachon ne Diwali ka tyohar manate hue kaha, "Kash kal chutti hoti. Kya hum kal school nahi jaayein? " Mummy papa hasein aur bole, "Chor Chor mausere bhai."

While celebrating Diwali, kids said, "We wish it was a holiday tomorrow. Can we skip school tomorrow?" Mom and Dad laughed and said, "Birds of a feather flock together!"

राई का पहाड़ बनाना
Raaee ka pahaad banaanaa
Making a mountain out of mustard seed
Meaning - To make a big issue out of a small thing
English Idiom - Making a mountain out of a molehill

जब आरव ने शरवी को भाईदूज पर राखी बांधी तो उसके दोस्त ने कहा, "अरे! लड़की को क्यों धागा बंद कर रहे हो?" आरव ने बोला, "बहन भी रक्षा कर सकती है। राई का पहाड़ मत बनाओ।"

Jab Aarav ne Sharvi ko Bhai Dooj par rakhi bandhi toh uske dost ne kaha, "Arre! Ladki ko kyon dhaga bandh rahe ho?" Aarav ne bola, "Behen bhi rakhsha kar sakti hai. Rai ka pahaad mat banao."

When Aarav tied Rakhi to Sharvi on Bhaidooj, his friend said, "Hey! Why are you tying the thread to a girl?" Aarav said, "Sister can also protect. Don't make a mountain out of a molehill."

आसमान से गिरे खजूर में अटके

Aasmaan se **gire**, **khajoor** mein **atke**
Fell from **sky**, **stuck** in **dates**
Going from one problem into another
English Idiom - Out of the frying pan into the fire

राजू की माँ ने कहा, "दिवाली ख़तम हो गयी। चलो अब क्रिसमस के लिए सफाई चालू करते हैं।" राजू बोला, "आसमान से गिरे, खजूर में अटके।"

Raju ki maa ne kahaa, "Diwali khatam ho gayi. Chalo ab Christmas ke liye safaaii chalu kartein hain." Raaju bola, "Aasmaan se gire, khajoor mein atke."

Raju's mom said, "Diwali is done. Now let's start cleaning to prepare for Christmas. Raju said, "Jumped out of the frying pan into the fire."

बीरबल की खिचड़ी
Birbal ki khichadi
Birbal's khichadi
Meaning - Something that takes way too long and may not end also
English Idiom - Never-ending

पापा ने कहा, "कब से बच्चे कमरे में बैठे क्रिसमस के उपहार तैयार कर रहे हैं। बीरबल की खिचड़ी पका रहे हैं क्या?"

Papa ne kahaa, "Kab se bacche kamre mein baithe Christmas ke uphaar taiyaar kar rahe hain hain. Birbal ki khichadi pakaa rahe hain kya?"

Father said, "Since when the kids are inside the room wrapping their presents for Christmas. Are they writing a never ending story?"

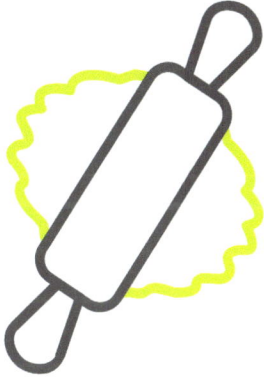

पापड़ बेलना

Paapad belna
To roll Paapad
Meaning - To put in extraordinary efforts to achieve something
English Idiom - Bend over backwards

पिताजी को क्रिसमस के लाइट्स सुलझाने के लिए बहुत पापड़ बेलने पड़े।

Pitaji ko Christmas ke lights suljhaane ke liye bahut paapad belne pade.

Father had to bend over backwards to detangle the Christmas lights.

अब पछताए होत क्या जब चिड़िया चुग गई खेत

Ab pachchtaaye hot kya, jab chidiya chug gayi khet
Why regret once bird has eaten the whole field

Meaning - To feel sorry or sad about something that has happened
English Idiom - To cry over spilled milk

डोनट का डब्बा खाली देखकर दिवा रोने लगी। माँ ने कहा, "अब पछताए होत क्या, जब चिड़िया चुग गई खेत।"

Donut ka dabba khaali dekh, Diva ro di. Ma ne kaha, "Ab pachtaaye hot kya, jab chidiyaa chug gayi khet."

Seeing the donut box empty, Diva started crying. Mother said, "It's no use crying over spilled milk."

अंत भला तो सब भला

Ant bhalaa toh sab bhalaa

When end is well, all is well

Meaning - When something ends well inspite of troubles

English Idiom - All's well that ends well.

त्योहारों की भाग दौड़ के बाद सबको लगता है कि अंत भला तोह सब भला।

Tyohaaron ki bhaag daud ke baad sabko lagta hai ki ant bhala toh sab bhala.

When all the festivities' running around is over, everyone feels all's well that ends well.

Tips for Teaching or Learning Conversational Hindi

Hindi is one of the most popular languages in the world, with nearly 1.5 billion speakers. Here are six simple strategies you can use -

- Start practicing some basic questions and answers in Hindi right away. *How are you? What's your name? Where are you going? Did you eat? etc.* are great examples

- Learning a new set of alphabets/scripts will take time. The **Ka Kyaa Kare** picture book is a great simple introduction to Hindi speaking, using daily situations and sentences we speak daily.

- Don't be afraid to make mistakes. Everyone is often worried about embarrassing themselves but when you try to learn a language, everyone will appreciate you, even for trying. No matter what your age.

- Watch content in the Hindi language. Repeatedly. The mistake we often make is to keep looking for new content every day, but repetition is key, so find a show you like, watch is again and again and use the sentences, jokes, etc, in your daily lives.

- Find ways and reasons to use the language. English is quite common; often, people, especially kids, do not feel the need to speak their native language. Immersing yourself in situations where Hindi speaking is common is a great way to hold yourself accountable and help kids see the advantages. **Ameya's Two Worlds** picture book does a great job of helping kids see how speaking Hindi or any native language can be a superpower.

- Get help from the community and family. Family and friends all speak English. Encourage them to hold you or your child accountable by providing a safe space to speak the language.

Ka Kyaa Kare is a practical alphabet book that helps with pronunciation and simple phrases used in daily life.

Ameya's Two Worlds is set in a vibrant Indian wedding that helps everyone see what a blessing being multilingual can be.

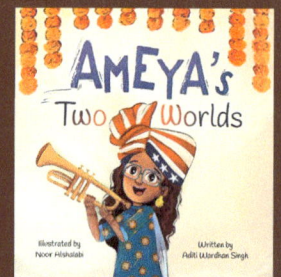

About the Author

Aditi Wardhan Singh is a multi-award-winning, bestselling author of eleven inclusive books rooted in modern values and heritage. She founded **RaisingWorldChildren.com**, an in-print and online collaborative platform for diverse voices. Raised in Kuwait, Aditi knows first hand the need for stories that help with bullying prevention, self-confidence and identity development for third culture kids. In her spare time she teaches dance, Hindi and creative writing.

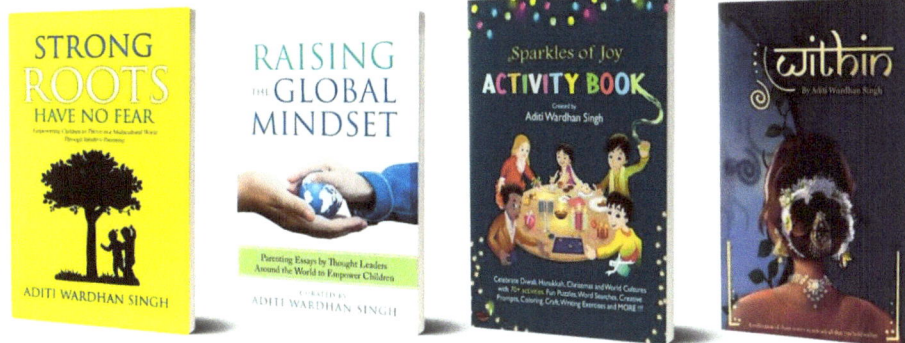

Thank you for taking a moment to review this book on Amazon or GoodReads. Get FREE festive activity sheets, comprehensive guide to festivals from India that elaborate on the traditions shown in these pages, classroom guide and audio-video versions of this book on **RaisingWorldChildren.com**